HOW TO WRITE

AND OTHER
SHORT POEMS

D0039158

HOW TO WRITE

Haiku

AND OTHER
SHORT POEMS

by Paul B. Janeczko

Scholastic Inc.

New York   Toronto   London   Auckland   Sydney
Mexico City   New Delhi   Hong Kong   Buenos Aires

ISBN 0-439-40964-0

12 11 10 9 8 7 6 5 4 3 2   4 5 6 7 8 9/0

Printed in the U.S.A.   40
First printing, May 2004

WELCOME

I don't know if you've written much poetry. Maybe you have. Maybe you haven't. But perhaps you've just decided that you're ready to try writing poetry. Good for you! The important thing is that you've picked up this book and you want to explore writing haiku, tanka, and other forms of short poetry. It's okay if you're nervous about what other people will say. The good news is that you never have to show your poems to anyone. Consider Emily Dickinson. She wrote hundreds of small poems on scraps of paper and, with a few exceptions, never showed them to a single person. Today, she is one of the most admired poets in the world.

The point of writing poetry is not to become famous. (Trust me.) Or even to get your poems published. The point of writing poetry is to capture your experiences and feelings in the best possible words. Writing poetry lets you experiment with that wonderful thing called language. It gives you a chance to record your life, the good parts as well as the bad parts, on paper.

Some people choose to write haiku, tanka, or clerihew because they think it's easy. I mean, how hard can it be to write a short poem? Well, I have news for them. Writing a good short poem is challenging *because* it uses only a handful of words. But I hope that the instructions and suggestions in this guide will help you write good short poems.

The first part of the book is devoted to haiku and related forms, like tanka and senryu. I've also included suggestions for writing "fun haiku" and *renga*, or linked poems. The second part of the book explores three short, rhyming, and often humorous poetic forms: clerihew, limerick, and synonym poems. You can skip over the first part of this guide and start reading the section on limericks. But I suggest you start at the beginning and work your way through the book. Many of the poetic concepts you'll learn in the section on haiku — like word choice, details, and economy of language — are equally important in the poetic forms in the second part of the guide. But no matter how you use this guide, I hope it helps you have fun with language as you develop as a poet.

INTRODUCTION

It's challenging to write a good haiku. Think about it: You need to capture a scene or an experience in seventeen syllables — that's maybe a dozen words. And not just any words will do. Your poem should use vivid and expressive words. It may seem easy. But as you begin to write haiku, you'll find that writing a good one requires many skills. Read these two samples:

Tonight the weather
will be downright nasty with
more rain tomorrow

My dog is a white
poodle that enjoys barking
when I try to sleep

Each group of lines *looks* like a haiku. In fact, if you count the syllables, you'll find that each "poem" contains seventeen syllables, arranged in lines of 5–7–5 syllables, just like a haiku. The truth is, however, that neither group of words is a haiku. They're only statements of fact or opinion.

Haiku are much more than that. Working hard to write a great haiku will give you a tremendous sense of accomplishment. And if you feel like it, you can even share your haiku with a friend. (In fact, I will suggest ways to do just that later in this guide.) Or you can treat each short poem as a gem that you prefer to put away in a safe place.

If you've never written a poem in your life, don't fret. In many ways, writing haiku is a good way to begin writing poetry. As you work your way through this guide, you will learn about:

- paying attention.
- creating images with your words.
- using only the best words in your poem.
- writing with economy.

These are all skills that will serve you well as a poet, no matter what kind of poetry you write. Let me explain.

PAYING ATTENTION

We live in a very busy world. Instant world-wide communication bombards us with information. There's fast food and e-mail. Our crammed schedules are often impossible to maintain. It's difficult to slow down and notice things. But one of the great things about poetry, whether we're reading it or writing it, is that it gives us the opportunity to do just that: to slow down and notice the world around us. In fact, one reason I always write the first few drafts of my poems in longhand rather than on the computer is because writing by hand slows me down. On the computer, I could easily type sixty or seventy words a minute. But when I write a poem, I don't *want* to write sixty or seventy words a minute. The whole poem might be only twenty or fifty words, and I want to pay attention to every one.

Writing poetry all starts with paying attention. If you are serious about writing poetry, you need to slow down and observe. Only when you pay attention to the world around you will you be able to capture in words what you see, hear, and feel. If you have a notebook handy, you'll be able to jot down some words or maybe even a quick draft of a poem.

CREATING IMAGES

We usually think of an image as something we see. But an image can be much more. An image often makes use of more than one sense. An image may involve something you hear. For example, you might write about the sounds of your baby brother singing nonsense sounds as he lies in his crib. Or you might write about a horrible storm and how the wind roared like a freight train. These are, in a sense, images created by sounds you've heard. When you observe and when you write, be aware of your senses — sight, sound, smell, taste, and touch — and jot down words that will use these senses to create an image for your reader.

USING ONLY THE BEST WORDS

English poet Samuel Taylor Coleridge once described poetry as using "the best possible words in the best possible order." While I don't know that you can (or should) define poetry, I do believe that this description is true. And the best words will not always be the first words that you come up with. In fact, the best words often come later in the writing process, after you have had a chance to rewrite and perhaps get some feedback from a writing partner. You might also get help in finding the right word from a dictionary or a thesaurus. But you might also capture the right word by paying attention to conversations, reading lots of poems, and experimenting with words.

WRITING WITH ECONOMY

No matter what kind of poems you write, a successful poem is economical with words. This means that you won't use six words when you can cut out the flab and keep the three or four most precise words. In some ways, haiku is "extreme" poetry. In seventeen syllables, which is maybe a dozen words or so, you must present a scene for a reader. Talk about economy! As you work on your haiku, particularly when you revise, keep a sharp pencil handy and be on the lookout for words that can be cut from your poem. Keep only the best words.

A FEW WORDS ABOUT THE WRITING PROCESS

No doubt your teachers have told you a lot about the writing process. They probably explained the steps involved — brainstorming, drafting, revising, proofreading, and publishing — and encouraged you to follow these steps. I think that's good advice. But you also need to remember that the writing process is different for everyone. For example, it might take you more time to brainstorm a good idea than it takes your friend. Or you might write a better first draft than your friend, so you need to spend less time on revising. The whole point of the writing process is for you to think carefully while you write and not settle for the first idea that falls out of your head and onto the page.

When I make author visits to schools, students and teachers frequently ask me if I follow the steps in the writing process. I tell them that I do . . . generally. But the process is different for me depending on what book I'm writing. For example, with some of my books, I spend a lot of time brainstorming before I get an idea that really excites me. (I love this step of the process, by the way, because anything goes!) Some of my books require more editing and revising than others. So not only will the process be different from writer to writer, but the process may vary from project to project. Just remember that the point of the writing process is to get you to think carefully as you write. Take your time. Let the ideas percolate in your mind — and on the pages of your notebook. Carefully consider the words you will use. Use only the best, most expressive words. You might be so excited about your writing assignment that you barrel through the first draft. Fine. Just make sure that you go through the revising and proofreading steps in slow-motion. Never hand in an assignment — whether it is a book report, a short story, or a poem — until it is as good as you can get it. Nobody wants to read a piece of writing that's not your best effort.

Just in case you aren't clear about what the writing process involves, here's a brief review of the steps.

BRAINSTORMING

This is when you let your imagination fly. As I said, anything goes. Nobody is going to grade your brainstorming, so don't try to get it "right." Just get it down on paper. You'll fix it later. This book is about writing short poems. You don't need to brainstorm them the way you would a short story, for which you need to consider characters, setting, plot, and so on. To brainstorm for a short poem, you will spend time observing and taking notes.

DRAFTING

Once you've made your observations and taken notes, you're ready to put them down on the page in a way that follows the structure of whatever poetic form you're writing. Because these poems are so short, you can make three or four drafts of the same poem before you settle on the one that you think is the best.

REVISING

I have learned over time — and with the help of a stack of rejected manuscripts — that the only way to get my writing to be the best it can be is to revise and rewrite again and again, as many times as it takes to get it the way I want it. There's really no way around it.

PROOFREADING

A lot of young writers I know tend to move too quickly through this step of the writing process, even though it is as important as the other steps. Take your time and carefully proof-read. Make sure you use the spell-check program on your computer. Keep a thesaurus handy so you can replace any vague or boring words that slipped into your poems. Always read your poems out loud and often during the process. You'll be surprised at how many mistakes you will catch when you read your poems aloud. Remember, this is the last step before you write your final copy for publication. Take your time with it.

PUBLISHING

Without a doubt, this is one of the most re-warding parts of writing. When I get the first copy of my newest book, it's very exciting. But I have "published" my work in other ways, like faxing a new poem to my wife at work or writing a funny poem on a card and sticking it in my daughter's backpack. If you've worked as hard as you can on a poem, you'll be anxious to share it with someone. And that's a great feeling.

BEFORE YOU START WRITING

With some effort and practice, you'll be writing good short poems before too long. As with any skill, practice helps. So, as you begin reading this guide, make a pledge to yourself that you will practice your writing and not give up when you write a handful of mediocre poems. The good poems will come *if* you practice. But I suspect that you'll find yourself enjoying the practice as you see your skill as a poet improve.

What tools will you need? Any poet needs the hardware and software discussed below.

A POET'S HARDWARE

A writer's notebook. It's a no-brainer that a writer's notebook is a must. But you'd be surprised at how many people don't bother to use a notebook to save all their notes, ideas, and scribblings. Buy one that you like because you'll use it often. Your notebook should have pages that are about 8" x 10". I'd advise against a smaller notebook for your main notebook because smaller pages may cramp your style. Many people like spiral notebooks because they lie flat when you're writing. Some writers like the fact that they can flip back the pages of a spiral notebook and see just the page they're writing on. I prefer the hard-cover notebooks with the marbled cover. But the choice is yours.

A pocket notebook. Yes, I know that in the previous paragraph I advised against a smaller notebook. But a pocket notebook is for you to carry around, maybe in your back pocket or in your purse. This small notebook is where you write the notes and observations that come to you when you don't have your writer's notebook with you. Let's say you've just gotten off the bus and you notice the wind blowing through the trees and whipping the flags that are hanging outside many of the houses on your street. This would be the perfect time to take out your pocket note-book and jot down exactly what you see and feel. Later that night, you can transfer those notes to your writer's notebook.

In addition to being able to jot down notes, your pocket notebook is a place where you can write drafts of your poems. Because the poems discussed in this guide are short, they will fit perfectly on a small sheet of paper.

You might even want to get a second pocket notebook, as I did. In addition to saving all my completed poetry on my computer's hard drive, I also write down each poem in a pocket notebook. Because I have large handwriting, I simply turn the notebook sideways and write each poem on a separate page.

In Your Notebook

Without giving much thought to writing a poem, take either of your notebooks on a test-drive and write down some observations. What should you write? Things you notice. Look in your backyard and jot down what you see. Or sit in a park and observe. What do you notice? What do you hear? Just take notes. Don't worry about being perfect. Just remember to be as exact and specific as you can.

Pens, pencils, and markers. If you were to visit my office, one of the first things you'd probably notice is that I'm wild about pens. I like pens and markers of all sorts and prices. Pencils? I can't stand them. But give me a good pen — preferably an old-fashioned fountain pen or a felt-tip marker with a thick point — and I'm one happy writer. I don't expect you to get carried away with pens the way I do. However, I would suggest that you get yourself a pen that feels comfortable, as well as a bunch of markers for adding some color to your notebooks. A couple of highlighters would also be a good idea so you can emphasize words, phrases, and ideas in your notes that you want to remember.

Dictionary and thesaurus. It goes without saying, but I'll say it anyway: Anyone serious about becoming a better writer needs to have a dictionary and a thesaurus close at hand. They are invaluable tools. And the good part is that it won't cost you a fortune to buy good paperback editions of these reference books. You can buy both of these books for about the cost of a CD. Chances are, your computer has a dictionary and a thesaurus loaded in its software. That's great. But computer editions of these books aren't going to help when you are writing in the backyard or in the park and you need to look up a word. Do yourself a favor and invest in a paperback dictionary and thesaurus to keep on your desk or to toss into your backpack when you're going to write away from your desk.

Collections of poetry. Although you need to be a reader if you want to be a writer, I will save my reading suggestions until the end of this section. You'll be better off if you try to write your own poetry before you read what other poets have published. One haiku poet said that the best haiku are written by beginners or by masters with years of experience. I'm guessing that you fit into the first category, so this guide should be just the thing for you. But after you've written some poetry, you might want to visit the library and check out a poetry anthology. By reading poetry, you will learn a lot about its possibilities.

A POET'S SOFTWARE

Quiet time. If you're at all like my daughter, who's an eighth grader, you like to do your homework with music blaring from your CD player while you're talking on the phone and watching an episode of your favorite TV show. Now I'll be the first to admit that I always have music playing when I work. But it's generally soft, quiet music that doesn't distract me from my work. So my advice is this: When it comes time to write poetry, try to find some peace and quiet. You don't have to lock yourself away for a weekend. But if you can set aside 20–30 minutes of quiet time for writing, it will serve you well. In that quiet, you can better visualize the scene in your poem, and you can concentrate on the words that you'll need to craft your poem. If 20–30 minutes sounds like it's beyond your endurance, try 10 or 15 minutes. If you need to have music playing, keep it very low. Who knows? You may even get to like a little peace and quiet. Stranger things have happened.

The right attitude. Peace and quiet might give you a hint about the attitude you need to write good poetry. You need to give yourself the chance to closely observe your world. It doesn't matter if you live in an apartment on a busy street in a noisy city or on a quiet winding road in the country. Your world will be the subject of your poetry. It's hard to pay attention when you are being distracted by your favorite CD cranking in the background or your friends telling you the latest gossip. I know you think it doesn't affect you, but it does. If you really want to write poetry, you need to be ready to concentrate.

An eye for details. All good writing, especially poetry, relies on details. This is especially true with haiku because you have only seventeen syllables to say what you need to say. The words you choose must be the best words to capture the scene that you are writing about. I'll say more about this later, but remember to be on the lookout for details. No detail is too small to consider for your poem. If you pay attention in a quiet, mindful way, you'll notice those details.

In Your Notebook

Take a look at the observations I asked you to write in your notebook on page 15. Read them carefully and see if you notice any spots where you could have been more specific. For example, did you say *bird* instead of *blue jay* or *crow*? Do you notice some verbs that can be sharper? Instead of *went*, could you write *sprinted, walked,* or *darted* instead? Change any vague words to something more specific.

Write with a Partner

Although I am a firm believer in having peace and quiet when you write, sometimes it can be helpful to speak with someone about your work. A writing partner could read your drafts and give suggestions. But she might also be able to offer an opinion when you ask a question about a poem. For example, you can ask, "Does this poem sound better *this* way or *that* way?" And with some of the poetic forms that I explore later in this guide, you and your partner can actually work together on a poem. Try to think of someone who might be a good writing partner for you. Perhaps you can return the favor to that person.

HAIKU

HOW HAIKU HAPPENED

In a way, haiku began as a party game. In thirteenth-century Japan, it was common for people to gather at parties and compose a long collaborative poem called a renga ("linked poem"). Here's how they played the game: A poet started the renga with a three-line poem called a *hokku.* This opening trio of lines was very important because it established the setting of the poem, especially the time. Rather than stating specifically when the poem was taking place, the more skilled poets would include a seasonal word, called the *kigo.* The poet could, for instance, use a kigo like *snow, frigid wind,* or *ice* rather than, say, *winter* or *December.* (As you will later learn, the seasonal word is still an important part of haiku.)

Once a poet had written an opening hokku, the next person contributed two lines to respond to the opening lines. The next person would contribute three lines, the next poet another two lines, and so on for the remainder of the renga, which could wind up containing a hundred verses, or links. Except for the opening hokku, the poem was made up on the spot and became something of a dialogue composed by many poets.

If you considered yourself a poet and were invited to a renga party, you went to the party prepared with several opening hokku, hoping that you would be selected to start the renga. These opening lines were usually the best-known part of the renga. Many people might not have been very familiar with the rest of the poem — much the way many people know the first verse and chorus of a popular song, but hardly anyone knows the verses that come next. Take, for example, the popular children's song "Pop! Goes the Weasel." Most people know the first verse:

All around the mulberry bush,
The monkey chased the weasel.
The monkey thought t'was all in fun,
Pop! Goes the weasel.

But how many know what comes after that? Not many people. Not me, in fact, until I looked it up:

Rufus has the whooping cough,
Poor Sally has the measles.
And that's the way the doctor goes,
Pop! Goes the weasel.

Because many poets came to renga parties with a handful of opening hokku and only one was needed per renga, most poets went home with leftover three-line poems. Over time, as the renga declined in popularity, poets began to publish their opening verses as individual poems. These new poems were called haiku. There are four poets who are considered masters of the Japanese haiku: Basho (1644–1694), Buson (1716–1784), Issa (1763–1827), and Shiki (1867–1902). It is believed that Shiki first used the term haiku in the late 1800s. You'll see their work later in this guide.

THE BASICS OF HAIKU

What are some of the things that go into a good haiku? Most people agree that the heart is what's called *the haiku moment.* This is when you are so struck by a scene — like snow covering apple trees — or an event — such as hearing a flock of geese — that you can't help but want to share it with someone. The haiku moment has a "whoa!" quality to it. You are so taken by the scene that you may literally stop in your tracks. Whoa! If someone were with you, you might have said, "Did you see *that*?!" The haiku moment happens quickly. That's why it's not called the "haiku hour." It's a moment. We need to pay attention or we will miss such moments.

So you have experienced a haiku moment. What's next? Well, if you jotted down some impressions of your experience, try to recreate them in a haiku. What qualities does a haiku have? If it were a machine, you might say that it had three parts: a time, a place, and an event or scene. A haiku is about one moment. It's not about a baseball game or a hike you took in the woods. The game and the hike are not moments. Your haiku might be about a moment in the baseball game. Maybe that instant was when the sun slid behind the scoreboard. It's about a haiku moment on the hike. Maybe you noticed an aster that was growing out of a crack in a chunk of granite. When you write your haiku, make sure it's about one scene or event. In other words, think small.

In Your Notebook

Since writing about a haiku moment is so important to good haiku, see if you can recall haiku moments in your life. You might not be able to recall them in enough vivid details to write a haiku about them, but thinking about such moments and jotting them down in your notebook may help prepare you for other haiku moments. If you think you can, write a haiku about one of these past moments. Give it a try!

Now that you have a basic idea of what a haiku is, let me list some of the basic elements of haiku. After I do that, I'll explain each element and give you some examples to illustrate each part. Keep in mind that you will run across some haiku that do not follow all of the "rules." That's okay. Any good poet will tell you that after you have mastered the rules of a poetic form, you can experiment with it. I'll say more about that later, too. Take a look at the elements of haiku listed below. You may notice that they deal with structure, content, and language.

CHECKLIST OF HAIKU INGREDIENTS

* A haiku is a three-line poem made up of seventeen syllables.
* The syllables in a haiku are arranged with five syllables in the first line, seven in the middle line, and five in the third line.
* There are frequently two beats or stressed syllables in the first line, three in the second line, and two in the final line.
* There is a pause after the fifth syllable or after the twelfth syllable. In other words, at the end of the first or second line.
* A haiku is written in the present tense. It is happening *now*. It is about a haiku moment.
* A haiku will tell the where, when, and what of the haiku moment.
* A haiku includes a seasonal word.
* A haiku creates an image of *one* thing.
* A haiku describes, but doesn't explain.

You're probably thinking, "How could there be so many rules for such a little poem?" Don't worry. You'll see that most of these elements are simple, and as you begin writing your own haiku, you'll notice that you include these elements without giving them much thought. Trust me.

Since it's wise to learn from the masters, I'll use haiku by Issa, Basho, Buson, and Shiki to illustrate what goes into writing a good haiku. The first thing you'll notice about their haiku is that not a single one of them follows the 5–7–5 syllable count. One of the reasons for this is that these poems are translated from Japanese, which has a different structure than English. Don't worry about that. Instead, remember that the *spirit* of the haiku is more important than strictly keeping to seventeen syllables. By "spirit of the haiku" I mean, of course, trying to write a poem that captures the haiku moment. And these poets did just that. For now, we'll forget about syllable count and look at other elements of their haiku.

Blown from the west,
fallen leaves gather
in the east.

Buson

Crescent moon —
bent to the shape of
the cold

Issa

The hollyhocks
lean toward the sun
in the May rain

Basho

A lightning flash:
between the forest trees
I see water

Shiki

Once you have read these haiku, reread them. Take your time. You might notice some of these qualities:

1. All of the poems are **written in the present tense**. They are happening now. Any of these poets could be writing about an incident that happened yesterday, last week, or last year. But they write as if the incidents were happening now.

2. Each haiku **describes one moment**. Read the poems again and see if you can describe in a few words the haiku moment that each poet talks about. Jot down your answers in your notebook.

3. Do these haiku include a **slight pause after the fifth or twelfth syllable**? Since many haiku — like these, for example — do not strictly follow the 5–7–5 pattern, you should look for the break at the end of the first or second line. Read the haiku again and see if you notice at the end of which line the pause occurs. You can write your opinion in your notebook.

4. All the poems contain a **seasonal word**. That word might be an obvious word or phrase like *spring snow*. But more often it will be a subtle reference to a season. In which season do these haiku take place? Carefully reread the poems and see if you can tell.

Now turn to page 130 to check your answers.

SEEING THE PROCESS

You might think that there are a lot of things to remember when you write a haiku. Well, yes and no. Yes, you should be familiar with the ingredients that go into a good haiku. But no, you don't need to clutter your mind trying to remember all of them while you're wandering around waiting to stumble upon a haiku moment. Just be alert and open to the haiku moment. Carry a notebook and pencil with you, so when you do experience a haiku moment, you can jot down some notes. Maybe you can even scribble down a quick draft of your poem. That would be a great way to start writing your haiku.

When you get back to your desk and writer's notebook, you can take your notes, observations, and draft, and begin to revise your poem. That's the real work of writing a haiku (or any poem, for that matter): rewriting it until you get it exactly how you want it.

Let me show you how I came to write one of my haiku. Seeing the process that I went through might help you when you write your poems. My haiku moment happened one morning last November after a snow that came a few weeks earlier than usual. I had just dropped off my daughter at school and noticed on the drive home the snow clinging to the limbs of the apple trees in the orchard near our house. I pulled off the road and scribbled some notes in the pocket notebook I keep in my car. Here's what I wrote:

November
first snow
apple trees
blossom
bloom
hanging off branches
branches covered with snow

When I got home, I grabbed a pad, sat at my office desk, and started scribbling my draft. I fought the urge to write a perfect poem. It was, after all, the earliest of drafts. I wound up writing things like:

The apple trees look like they are in blossom
The snow looks like apple blossoms
The apple trees are blooming snow

Not great poems, I know, but that's okay. A first draft is supposed to give you the chance to get your ideas down on the page. Any idea is worth writing down. Remember that the writing process has one important part that can help you write a better poem: revision. That's when the real writing happens. But you can't revise if you don't have a draft.

After looking at my notes and my drafts, I tried again and came up with this:

Rows of apple trees
in blossom
in November snow

Better than my drafts, but still not as good as I wanted the poem to be. After more revising and tinkering, I wound up with a haiku that I was pretty happy with:

November snow . . .
rows of apple trees
blossom

As I read it over, I looked to see how well I had followed in the tradition of the haiku masters. I had focused on a small scene. My syllable count was off, but I did include the what, where, and when of the haiku moment. The poem did have a noticeable line break at the end of the first line. I included a seasonal word. I liked best the way I brought together in one poem two contrasting images: the snow and the apple trees. Overall, I thought I had captured the spirit of the haiku.

To help you write good haiku and other short poems, I have included "Improve Your Craft" sections throughout this book. These are exercises that are tied to important aspects of good poetry. Take your time with these exercises. Write them in your notebook. And remember that you are not trying to find "right" and "wrong" answers. You are looking for ways to write better poetry.

LOOKING AT ART

Since the whole point of haiku is to capture the haiku moment, it might seem silly to look at pictures in books and write haiku about them. But there is the possibility that an illustration in a book can trigger a haiku moment. I'm talking about the glorious pictures you might find in a book of paintings by one of the masters, like Vincent van

Gogh, Winslow Homer, or Georgia O'Keeffe. You could also look through books of photographs by Ansel Adams, Margaret Bourke-White, or Dorothea Lange. And even if you don't have a haiku moment while you are looking at their pictures, you can use them to practice describing scenes. You'll need to put yourself at the scene but not *in* the scene. Who knows? You might write some good haiku about the pictures you studied.

One advantage of writing a haiku about, say, a magnificent mountain range photograph by Ansel Adams is that you can take your time and study the scene as you write. The sunset you see this evening will be a one-of-a-kind experience. Tomorrow's sunset will be different. But with an Adams photograph in a book, you can come back to that same scene the following day or week and it will be exactly as it was when you left it. On the other hand, you might actually see the scene differently after you have written about it and not looked at it for a while. Another advantage of working from pictures in books is that you might be able to copy them and include them with haiku on greeting cards that you give to your family and friends.

If you decide that you want to look at pictures to give you ideas for haiku, look at the pictures carefully. What do you notice about them? What does the artist seem to highlight or emphasize? What feeling do you get from the picture? These are some of the same questions you can ask yourself when you write a haiku.

TAKING AN OBSERVATION WALK

Since good haiku reflect haiku moments, there's no substitute for being open to such moments and being ready to take notes when a haiku moment happens to you. Be aware of what is happening around you. If you have your pocket notebook with you, that's an obvious place to take notes. But when you are caught without that little helper, don't fret. Grab a scrap of paper and scribble your notes on it. The important thing is to capture the details of the moment.

You might also want to consider taking an observation walk with the specific intention of looking carefully at the world around you and taking notes on what you experience. Notice I said that you should take notes on what you *experience*, not simply what you see. Remember to let all your senses work for you. Be aware of what you hear. Do you hear birds? Loud trucks and buses? Water lapping on the shore? The snap of a basketball hitting the pavement? What do you feel? Are you walking barefoot on grass or are you running down the street in sneakers? Do you feel the wind blowing through your hair? Do you feel the rough surface of the chain-link fence around the playground?

As long as we're talking about senses, remember that you can experience more than one sense at the same time. For example, you might have your fingers hooked in the chain-link fence while you feel the wind blowing through your hair. Or you might hear your baby sister cry while you are looking at the full moon. Don't forget that a good haiku will more than likely have contrasting images, so be ready for that.

Don't expect (or even hope) that your haiku moment will go in a straight line. It might take a detour, and you need to be ready to go with that impulse. For example, you may have noticed how the winter night is filled with the smell of baking apple pie from the next apartment. You may want to write about that. But as you begin writing, you flash back to a scene in your grandmother's kitchen. You can picture her sitting at the table wearing slacks and a Mickey Mouse sweatshirt, holding a paring knife to peel apples. You can see the apple peels in a pile on the table. The old woman is humming a gospel hymn. And outside, snow has begun to fall. Suddenly, the haiku that you thought was going to be about the smell of apple pie has turned into a haiku about your grandmother making apple pie in the warm kitchen as the snow falls. Just remember to write it in the present tense.

IMPROVE YOUR CRAFT #1: Line Break

One of the characteristics of a good haiku is that it has a break, usually after the fifth or twelfth syllable — in other words, at the end of the first or the second line. This break is usually obvious when you read the poem aloud.

Here's an example: *melting snow the sun shines into the back of an empty truck*. When I read this line out loud, I can hear that there is a definite pause after the word *snow*. Even though *melting snow* has only three syllables, it sounds like it is the first line of the haiku. In fact, here is the way Cor van den Heuvel wrote his haiku:

melting snow
the sun shines into the back
of an empty truck

In Your Notebook

To give you a little practice on where a break should go, take a look at the lines that I have included below. Each is a haiku, but I have written each one as a single line of words. Carefully read each line. In fact, I suggest that you read them out loud. As you read, listen to where you take a slight pause. Chances are, that's where the break should go.

Her mailbox leans into the honeysuckle rusted
    and empty

Between the lace curtains the white cat's eyes
    follow a snowflake

after the storm I cannot find the snowman's
    eyes

When you know where the pause comes, write the haiku in your notebook the way you think the poet wrote it. I've included the poems on page 131 so you can check to see how you did, but don't look before you try to put in the breaks on your own.

IMPROVE YOUR CRAFT #2:
Syllable Count

Since counting syllables is important to a good haiku poet, this would be a good time to make sure you understand what a syllable is. Basically, it is the smaller part of a word — the groups of letters and sounds that make up a word. For example, the word *until* is made up of two syllables (or sounds): *un* and *til*. The word *telephone* has three syllables or sounds: *tel-e-phone*. Some of the syllables in a word are stressed, which means that you say that syllable with a little more emphasis. For example, in the word *until*, the second syllable (*til*) is stressed. The first syllable in the word *telephone* (*tel*) is stressed.

In Your Notebook

Divide these words into syllables and underline the syllable that is stressed. The answers start on page 131.

personal	almanac
encyclopedia	sing
window	selection
outstanding	ridiculous
superintendent	discovery
quick	return

IMPROVE YOUR CRAFT #3: Seasonal Words

Seasonal words will be different depending on where you live. For example, in Maine, where I live, seasonal words for winter include such words as *snow, ice, blizzard, frigid wind,* and *snowflake.* But those certainly would not be winter words for Southern California or Florida. What seasonal words apply to where you live? Insects and animals also help identify the season. In which season do you think the following haiku takes place?

In the empty church
at nightfall, a lone firefly
deepens the silence

Nick Virgilio

What's the season for this haiku?

Cold wind . . .
just-swept leaves
gusting back

Sharon Lee Shafii

Turn to page 132 for the answers.

In Your Notebook

Turn to two clean, facing pages in your notebook and write seasonal words across the top of the pages. Divide each page with a vertical line, which will give you four columns. Write the name of one of the seasons at the top of each column. Then begin to list words that you associate with a specific season where you live. If you have a friend or relative who lives in a different part of the world, share your list and ask that person to tell you which words don't apply to that season where he/she lives. Then ask for a few words that he/she associates with each season.

IMPROVE YOUR CRAFT #4:
Seeing the Images

Although a good haiku describes one scene or moment, it does more than just that. It often contains two images. And those images often contrast. Contradictory images can take a reader by surprise in much the same way that the poet was taken by surprise when he had his haiku moment.

What do I mean by contrasting images? Take a look at this haiku by Wally Swist and see if you can identify the contrasting images that he used in his poem:

opened so boldly
in spring snow
the red tulip

Did you notice the contrast between the red tulip and the white snow? That's exactly the sort of thing that I'm talking about. The poet has not only contrasted the red (of the tulip) and the white (of the snow), but he has also contrasted a flower, which is a sign of spring, with snow, which we associate with winter, when most flowers are dormant.

In Your Notebook

Here are three other haiku to explore. Read them a couple of times. In your notebook, briefly note the contrasts that you find in the poems.

Lightning flash
crows sitting under
the scarecrow

George Swede

It also rained
pink magnolia blossoms
upon the lawn

Bernard M. Aaronson

even the cellar rats
sleeping late
this snowy morning

Penny Harter

Can you see the contrasts in these haiku? In the first poem, the poet contrasts a couple of things. First, he contrasts the light of the flash of lightning with the darkness. He also contrasts the "crows sitting under / the scarecrow," a scene we don't often see since a scarecrow's purpose is to scare away crows. In the second poem, the poet contrasts the pink petals and the green grass of the lawn. There is a slight contrast in the mood in the third haiku as the poet compares cellar rats, normally thought to be hideous creatures, peacefully sleeping late as the quiet snow falls.

IMPROVE YOUR CRAFT #5:
Feelings in Haiku

Some people who write haiku think of their poems as still-life paintings or photographs. While a good haiku contains concrete details to create an image, the poem should be more than just a painting, no matter how gorgeous it may be. A good haiku should include some feelings, without going overboard and becoming merely sentimental.

Take a moment to read this haiku that I wrote a couple of years ago. In fact, read it a few times.

Stickball players shout
as moonlight floods their field
from curb to curb

As is the case with most haiku, this one presents a simple scene in simple language: A bunch of kids are playing stickball in the street in the moonlight. If you read the poem carefully, however, I hope you notice the feeling that I was trying to get across in the poem. First of all, the whole scene in the poem is enjoyable. Think of you and your friends playing a game you enjoy outside on a moonlit summer night. To get the idea across that the players are really "into" the game, I use the word *shout* at the end of the first line, which is, by the way, the turning point in the poem. The one-word feeling I wanted to include in this poem is *fun.*

When I was writing the poem, I didn't want it to be overly emotional or "mushy." Although some people think that an overly emotional poem is a good poem, this isn't the case. True, you want to have emotion in a good poem — no matter what kind of poem you are writing — but you must avoid going overboard.

As far as my haiku is concerned, I could have written a much more emotional and sentimental poem by saying something like:

*Kids enjoy
the best time of their lives playing
stickball at night*

Or:

*Moonlight covers
the laughing kids playing
stickball in the street*

Part of the reason these examples are not good haiku is because they are too emotional. If you look more closely at these haiku, you will notice other reasons why they are not good poems. For one thing, neither has a balance point in the poem. There is no pause at the end of the first or second line. They explain rather than describe. Also, the language in these examples is not the precise language that you expect in a haiku. Notice in my "real" haiku that I use the word *floods* to show what the moonlight is doing. Notice, too, that I use the phrase *curb to curb* rather than *in the street.*

When you write your haiku, remember that you want to include feelings, but you don't want to overdo it and fall into sentimentality. The reader should know your feelings about the scene or event without being *told* how you feel. Your poem should suggest the feeling.

In Your Notebook

Go to the library and check out a book of haiku. You can start by looking for the books that I list on page 59, but any book of haiku will do. Read some haiku until you find a poem that you like very much. Copy it into your notebook. Below the poem, write a sentence or two that describes how you feel when you read the poem. Copy a few more poems that you like and write a little about how you feel when you read these poems.

IMPROVE YOUR CRAFT #6:
The What, Where, and When of Haiku

A good haiku will more than likely contain three elements: *what*, *where*, and *when*. To see what I mean, read this haiku by Ross Figgins a couple of times and see if you can identify the *what*, *where*, and *when*.

49

autumn shadows —
the scarecrow bends forward
closer to the earth

This haiku describes the scarecrow's shadow (*what*) in a field (*where*) during autumn (*when*). Bear in mind that the *what*, *where*, and *when* may not always be as cut and dry as they are in this poem. Nonetheless, you should be able to get a sense of these elements in a good haiku. And as a writer, you should make sure that your haiku contain these elements. At the same time, be careful not to make your poems too mechanical and predictable. No one wants to read a series of haiku in which the *what* always comes first and is always followed by the *where* and the *when*. Remember, too, that a good poem suggests, so these three elements need not always be obvious.

In Your Notebook

Here are three haiku that I used earlier in this book. Read through them a couple of times, copy them into your notebook, and identify the *what, where,* and *when.* You might want to highlight these elements using different-colored highlighters. Remember, the *what, where,* and *when* may not always be specifically stated. In that case, write your observations below each poem.

*Lightning flash
crows sitting under
the scarecrow*

George Swede

*It also rained
pink magnolia blossoms
upon the lawn*

Bernard M. Aaronson

even the cellar rats
sleeping late
this snowy morning

Penny Harter

The answers for this exercise are at the back of the book.

IMPROVE YOUR CRAFT #7:
Thinking Small

When you want to write a haiku about a scene, you need to remember to focus on a small part of what you see. As I said earlier, don't write a haiku about your backyard. Write one about the swing with a robin sitting on it or about the shovel that is standing alone in the garden. Don't write a haiku about the apartment building across the street. Instead, write about the sidewalk chalk drawing that is washing away in the rain or the violet petunias that are growing from a clay flowerpot on the fire escape. In other words, think small.

To help you think small, make a frame that you can use to view the world around you. To make your frame, you'll need a sheet of heavy paper — the heavier the paper, the stronger your frame will be. I like to use a file folder when I make a frame. You'll also need a ruler, pencil, and a pair of scissors.

To make the frame, draw a line two inches from each edge of the paper. All four lines should meet to make a smaller rectangle. When you are finished, your paper should look like this:

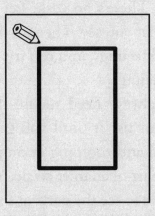

When you have drawn the lines of your frame, carefully cut out the center rectangle along the lines you've drawn. Your frame is ready to use!

How do you use the frame? Hold it at arm's length as you look at a scene and consider what you can see. For example, if you look at an apartment building through the frame, you won't see the whole building. You might see plants growing on the fire escape, or bright yellow curtains blowing in and out of one of the windows, or pigeons lined up on the edge of the roof. As a haiku poet, it's the small scene that should interest you.

Try looking at different scenes with your frame. But don't zoom from scene to scene as if you're filming an action movie. Take your time. Linger at various spots. Give yourself a chance to notice things. There's no rush. Let yourself have feelings for what you see. Then jot down your observations and feelings. You can try to make them part of your haiku.

Will you always need to use the frame? Of course not. But use it until you get the hang of thinking small and zooming in on particular images that are part of a larger scene. With practice, you will be able to see the parts of a scene that will be perfect for your haiku.

In Your Notebook

After you cut out the frame, try using it on a couple of scenes this way:

Examine a scene — say, the park down the street — without the frame. Look at the scene carefully. Then hold your frame at arm's length and look at the same scene again, *slowly* moving the frame as if you were looking though the viewfinder of a video camera. Look carefully. Chances are that you will notice more details when you use the frame. Write a few sentences about the differences you noticed.

After you've noted a couple of the differences, try the same exercise on a different scene. This time, write down some of the details that you noticed when you looked through the frame. When you have written down some good details, write a haiku about that scene.

IMPROVE YOUR CRAFT #8:
Experimenting with Form

Although the three-line haiku form that we know is the most widely used form, there are different ways to write the three-line haiku. Some writers prefer to have each line begin at the left margin. Others begin the first line at the margin, then tab in for the next line, then tab in twice for the third line as I did in this poem:

Stickball players shout
*   as moonlight floods their field*
*   from curb to curb*

As you become comfortable writing haiku, you might want to give some thought to other ways of writing your haiku. In fact, most Japanese haiku magazines and anthologies print each haiku as one vertical line of Japanese symbols. This is roughly equivalent to one line of English, like this poem by George Swede:

Dawn   only the mountain sees me leave

Here's another, this one by Marlene Mountain:

just enough rain to moisten the lips of the wild lily

You'll notice that Swede put in a couple of extra spaces after *Dawn* to let the reader know that there should be a slight pause after that word, as if it were the end of the first line of a three-line haiku. Other haiku poets, like Mountain, give no clue about where to pause, leaving it up to the reader, like this poem by Ruby Spriggs:

within closing petals silence

But if you read this poem carefully, you'll hear that there is slight pause after *petals*.

Some haiku is even written in two lines. Here's one example by Alan Pizzarelli:

the Ferris wheel turning
into the fog

These alternate forms of haiku demonstrate something that I said earlier in this guide: The form of the haiku is not as important as the *spirit* of the poem. When you write your haiku, don't be afraid to experiment and see what your poems look like if they are written on one line. You might decide that certain haiku look better that way, while others look more appealing in the more traditional form. It's up to you.

In Your Notebook

Take a look at a book of haiku from your school library. You'll notice that most of them are written in the traditional form: three lines, probably with each line indented a little bit farther than the line above it. Pick a haiku that you like and copy it over in your notebook, but do so in another form. In other words, can you see a different way of breaking up the poem? Don't be afraid to experiment with different arrangements. Do you notice how your new arrangement affects the way you read the poem? Does it affect how you feel about it?

BOOKS OF HAIKU

Visit your public library and see which books of haiku are in the collection. Chances are, you'll find a few anthologies of haiku that include the works of a number of poets. But while you're checking the library's catalog, see if there are any books by the four Japanese masters: Buson, Issa, Basho, and Shiki.

You can also check for these specific collections:

The Essential Haiku: Versions of Basho, Buson, and Issa. Robert Hass, editor. Ecco Press, 1994.

The Haiku Anthology. Cor van den Heuvel, editor. W.W. Norton & Company, 1999.

Haiku: Poetry Ancient and Modern. Jackie Hardy, editor. Tuttle Publishing, 2002.

Haiku Moment: An Anthology of Contemporary North American Haiku. Bruce Ross, editor. Tuttle Publishing, 1993.

Stone Bench in an Empty Park. Paul B. Janeczko, editor. Orchard Books, 2000.

As you read the poems in these anthologies, look for the elements of a good haiku in each one. But also look to see how the poets may have "broken the rules" and done something a little differently.

POEMS RELATED TO HAIKU

SENRYU

You may never have heard of the *senryu*. But once you try your hand at writing a senryu, the first cousin of the haiku, you'll be hooked. That's what happened to me. I'd been writing haiku and starting to feel that I was in a rut. Then a friend of mine sent me some senryu that he'd written. As soon as I read his poems, I cracked up and knew I had to try writing some of them.

Senryu started out as part of the renga that I mentioned earlier in this guide. They look like haiku but with one important difference: Instead of being about the nature that we experience around us, senryu are about human nature, the weird little quirks we have that make us human. And since senryu are witty and clever, I like to call them "haiku with an attitude."

If you read these senryu that I wrote, you will get the idea.

On Ferris wheel
  I regret french fries and milk shake . . .
    those below agree

Freedom vanishes
as the babysitter arrives . . .
kids are tied in nots

Toasted marshmallow
crisp and inviting skin:
inside burns your tongue.

You can see how the poems have the same characteristics of a haiku. They are three-line poems of seventeen syllables, divided into lines of five, seven, and five syllables. But you will notice one big difference, and that is the subject matter. Notice how these poems are about various attitudes and behaviors that make us human. One thing that doesn't change, however, is that you must remain true to the spirit of the poem and not be a slave to all those "rules" that I talked about earlier.

While a haiku captures a scene in nature, a senryu captures a scene from life. Don't try to tell a long story in your poem. Make it a very short story, but a story that shows something about human nature. For example, in my first senryu, I write of the regret of eating too much before going on the Ferris wheel.

Another thing you will notice in a senryu is that the slight pause in the poem is generally at the end of the second line. This makes the final line almost like the punch line of a joke. If you look at the Ferris wheel senryu again, my final line — *those below agree* — is a tag line to that story. I'm suggesting, of course, that when I get sick on the Ferris wheel, those below me also will wish that I'd not eaten fries and gulped a shake.

There's one more thing to keep in mind when you write your senryu. It is often based on a play on words. For example, look at the play on words in this senryu:

Mice dart in shadows
as barn cat waits and grins . . .
ah! fast food tonight

Can you see how I'm playing with the phrase *fast food*? Most people take it to be the food served at a drive-up burger restaurant. But in my poem, it refers to the mice zipping around in the barn.

There is also a play on words in my senryu about the babysitter: *Kids are tied in nots*. Notice how I spelled *nots*. It's not a misspelling. It's a play on the word *knot*, which is usually used in the expression *tied in knots* — and *nots* — which, of course, I mean to stand for all the things that the baby-sitter tells the kids *not* to do.

Even though the subject of a senryu is different from a haiku, the process of writing a senryu is the same. That means that you begin by observing and jotting down your observations in your notebook. What should you look for? Well, look for people being people. Look for things that show our human nature. Look for things that are contradictory, like the exercise fanatic who doesn't wear a seat belt or the girl who breaks up with her boyfriend and wails that she'll never find anyone else to love, only to walk hand in hand with a different boy by the end of science class!

I got the idea for my third senryu in this section last summer when some of my daughter's friends came to spend the night with us in a cottage we had rented for a few weeks. We were roasting marshmallows over a fire in the fireplace. One of the girls, who was not especially experienced with roasting marshmallows, was very pleased with the perfectly crisp skin on her marshmallow. Before anyone could warn her, she plucked the marshmallow off the tip of the stick and popped it into her mouth, only to immediately discover that the inside of the marshmallow was burning hot. I held that image until the girls went to sleep. Then I grabbed my pen and notebook, and scribbled it down. The next day I worked on the senryu.

When you write a senryu, you must be alert to human nature. You need to do some serious observing. Can you think of some good, safe places to observe life? Write down some ideas in your notebook. Places like the school cafeteria, the library, the mall, and the park work well. Be on the lookout for things that strike you as funny. Also look for things that are annoying about life, like dropping the soap when you are taking a shower and not being able to pick it up. Or squirting out way too much toothpaste and wishing you could get it back in the tube.

IMPROVE YOUR CRAFT: #9:
Brainstorming Your Senryu

I don't know about you, but I've wrecked more than a few writing projects by rushing through them thinking, "Oh, yeah, this is a fabulous idea!" only to discover that it wasn't as good as I'd thought. The problem was that I usually hadn't spent enough time developing the idea to make sure it would work. You can avoid that sort of calamity by taking your time in the brainstorming part of the writing process. Don't be afraid to fill your notebook with notes and lists and drawings and charts and diagrams, whatever will help you develop your ideas more fully before you start drafting.

Because the senryu is supposed to be humorous, you might want to take extra time brainstorming ideas. What sorts of things are funny? Are there different ways to approach a subject that might make it funnier? It might help to have a writing partner with a sense of humor like yours. On the other hand, if your writing partner has a sense of humor that is different from yours and you get a chuckle out of her with one of your ideas, that's great. When you brainstorm your senryu — by yourself or with a partner — remember that the whole point of brainstorming is to generate ideas. Not everyone is going to be a winner. Don't be afraid to be silly or outrageous. You can work out the details of your poem later as you write and revise it.

In Your Notebook

Another way to get ideas for your senryu is to think how you would complete these statements: *I hate it when . . . Did you ever notice how . . . I wonder what would happen if . . .* and *I can't believe that . . .* Divide a page in your notebook into quarters and write one of these phrases at the top of each section. Your page will look like this:

I hate it when . . .	Did you ever notice how . . .
I wonder what would happen if . . .	I can't believe that . . .

This diagram will help you keep these phrases in mind as you work your way through the day. Be on the lookout for things that can complete them. Write down your responses in your notebook.

Write with a Partner

From my experience of having students write senryu in my writing workshops, I've noticed that they sometimes write better poems when they work in pairs. Brainstorming with a partner is a great way to come up with exciting ideas for your poem. You and your partner could take turns using the prompts I gave above. For example, you might say, "I hate it when my sister keeps me up with her snoring." Maybe your partner might say, "Yeah, I know what you mean. I can hear my brother snoring right through the wall! It sounds like a chain saw." And, before you know it, you'll be off and running on some ideas that might turn into an hilarious senryu.

FUN HAIKU

While senryu are a legitimate form of haiku, other types of short, haikulike poems can be fun to write. These are not haiku, but they are sometimes called haiku because they follow the 5–7–5 format. Here are some examples of "fun haiku" written as if by a dog:

I hate my leash
Look, world, they strangle me! Ack
Ack Ack Ack Ack Ack!

I lie belly-up
In the sunshine, happier than
You ever will be.

I love my master:
Thus I perfume myself with
This long-rotten squirrel.

Here are some computer haiku. If you spend a lot of time with computers, you'll get a kick out of these. These haiku are really computer messages and warnings written in the form of a haiku.

The website you seek
Cannot be located but
Countless more exist.

Serious error.
All shortcuts have disappeared.
Screen. Mind. Both are blank.

Three things are certain:
death, taxes, and lost data.
Guess which has occurred?

Maybe your teachers could write their report comments in haiku:

It pains me to say:
Your son's tardies have earned him
Friday detention.

Or, maybe your parents could write you notes in the form of a haiku:

My grand love for you
does not stop me from saying:
Tonight is trash night.

Can you think of similar haiku that you could write? Maybe you can write one as if you were a cat. Of course, these are not true haiku even though they follow some of the conventions of haiku. Nonetheless, they are fun to write and perfect to share with your friends and relatives. Let your imagination go and have laughs writing some fun haiku.

IMPROVE YOUR CRAFT #10:
Keeping It Brief

Since one of the characteristics of a haiku — whether it is a traditional haiku or a fun haiku — is its brevity, it's a good idea to work on keeping your fun haiku short by trimming unnecessary words. Let me give you an example. Here's the haiku that appeared on page 70:

It pains me to say:
Your son's tardies have earned him
Friday detention.

As you probably know, that poem didn't start out that way. It started with a few words scribbled in my writer's notebook: *Friday detention for being late.* When I thought about what I wanted to say, I decided that I wanted the haiku to be a note from a teacher. I came up with this: *It bothers me to have to say this, but your son has detention on Friday because he's been late so many times.* You're right: It's way too long for a haiku. The first thing I did was to break it into lines to see what it looked and sounded like:

It bothers me to have to say this   [9 syllables]
but your son has detention on Friday   [10 syllables]
because he's been late so many times.   [9 syllables]

Still too long, but I had a better idea of what I was working with. Then I looked for words to cut out and words to change to make the poem fit the 5–7–5 haiku format. The first revision I made was to move *detention on Friday* to the last line, something like the punch line in a joke. After that, I cut down and changed some words until I wound up with the final poem. So, as you write and revise your fun haiku, look for ways to keep your poem short and funny.

In Your Notebook

Remember that your writer's notebook is an excellent place for you to jot down ideas. Be on the lookout for situations that could lead to some funny haiku. For example, what if the governor or the president issued statements in the form of a haiku? What if a referee issued fouls and warnings written in haiku?

Write with a Partner

It's no coincidence that much of the good writing on television or in the movies is done by a team of writers. The team may have only two writers. Maybe more. But it's common practice for comedy writers to work with someone so they can bounce ideas off each other. The same holds true for writing fun haiku.

Get together with your writing partner and see what hilarious ideas for fun haiku you can come up with. Make a list. When you have some good ideas, try them out in the haiku format and see what they look like. How do they sound? Even though these are fun haiku, you need to do your best to stick to the haiku format.

HAIBUN

While haiku is about a specific moment that made you stop and take notice, a *haibun* is the prose story that tells how you came to that haiku moment. The prose part of the haibun is autobiographical, which means that it is about something that happened to you or something you saw or did. As you will see below, the prose part of your haibun doesn't *explain* the haiku. The prose tells a story in which a haiku or two are important parts.

Here are parts of two haibun that show how autobiographical prose and haiku can work together. The first excerpt is by a man who is looking out his window.

I draw back the shades to reveal the mountain across the valley. The peak just begins to show a trace of redness. The sky to the west still contains stars dot-

ting the fading blackness. I drain the remaining
drops from a cup of green tea, and place it carefully
on the window ledge.

daybreak
all at once the absence
of stars

Turning from the window I take two steps
towards my cushion . . .

Gary Steinberg

In the next selection, called "Lunar Eclipse," a
man tells of a road trip he took with a friend.

My friend Frank and I are driving through a
snowstorm on the way to Bare Hill in hope of seeing
the total eclipse of the moon. The radio warns us
there is a travel advisory, and all unnecessary travel
is discouraged. We laugh a bit foolishly at this advice
coming over the airwaves.

snowstorm —
out of this eclipse night
only lunatics

Bare Hill, a place revered by the Seneca Indians, rises from the short of Canandaigua Lake into a large broad hill that overlooks the lake and the surrounding country. The sacredness of the hill, the chance that the storm front will move through, along with more than our fair share of dumb luck are what Frank and I are counting on in our quest to see the eclipse.

> *driving by faith . . .*
> *from the farmer's windblown field*
> *blinding snow*

Because of the storm we are running late . . .
Michael Ketchek

The haibun might especially interest you if you like to write stories about your life. If you've had to write autobiographical sketches for a language arts class, take a new look at them and see if you can find a spot or two where you could work in a haiku. If not, start from scratch and write a haibun.

IMPROVE YOUR CRAFT #11:
Using Details in Your Haibun

Any good writing, from a love letter to a thick novel, will include plenty of vivid details. If you are writing a thick novel, you'll use thousands of words, so you'll have lots of chances to include details to make your story come alive for the readers. But with a poem, you'll use only a few words. It's crucial that your details be specific and concrete.

Vivid details are grounded in the senses: sight, sound, smell, taste, and touch. In other words, you try to use words that appeal to one of the senses. Instead of saying *cat*, you might say *fat calico with one ear*, something that the reader can see. Instead of saying, *The thunder was loud*, you might say, *The thunder sounded like a cannon*, something that the reader can hear. Instead of saying, *The pancake tasted lousy*, you might say, *The pancake tasted like last week's gym socks.*

When you write a haibun, you'll need to revise it carefully to make sure that you've included details that appeal to the senses in the prose part and in the poetry parts of the piece.

In Your Notebook

Earlier, I suggested that you use your writer's notebook to save ideas and scenes that were part of your haiku moment. You might also give some thought to writing more about the circumstances that led up to your haiku moment.

Write with a Partner

Of all the poetic forms in this book, the haibun is one of the best suited for writing with a partner. One of the reasons is that the haibun has two parts to it, so one partner could write the prose narrative and the other could find a spot or two in the narrative where a haiku would work well. You could also work as a team writing both parts of the haibun. A third way that you might work with a partner is to find a piece of vivid prose narrative in a novel or a story and see if you can write a haiku or two that would fit smoothly into the story.

RENGA

As you know, haiku began as part of a long linked poem called a renga. It was not uncommon for many renga to be a hundred stanzas. Some of them, in fact, were even longer. One poet wrote a 5–7–5 stanza, which was linked by another poet who wrote a 7–7 stanza. The rest of the stanzas in the poem followed that pattern. "Eleven Hours" is an example of a renga that was written in English. (The names of the five poets who worked on the poem appear next to their contributions.) Here are the first 15 lines, which should give you a feel for the renga.

Eleven Hours

morning wind
blowing away the rain clouds
swaying willow buds

                              Philip Meredith

a group of children
getting on a tour bus

                    Tadashi Kondo

almost catching
never being caught
three boys and a duck
                    Robert Reed

shadows deepen
the old man locks the gate
                    Kris Young

crows gathering
in the branches
the sky darkens
                    Philip Meredith

in from the cold
the choir practices
                    Timothy Knowles

Can you see how the stanzas are linked? That doesn't mean that each one is strictly connected to all the other stanzas. But it does mean that taken together, they tell a story. In the case of "Eleven Hours," the story is about what goes on with a number of people in a period of time.

IMPROVE YOUR CRAFT #12:
Revising Your Renga

You already know how important revision is to a good piece of writing. Your poems will improve as your ability to revise improves. That might mean letting a friend read your poem to look for weak spots that you might have missed. It might mean putting the poem away and not looking at it for a couple of weeks, maybe longer. It might mean reading each revision out loud so you can really *hear* the words. Don't be shy about revising. It is one sure way to improve your writing.

Chances are that your renga will need some special revision because there are so many pieces to this linked poem. You need to make sure each section of the poem is good, of course, but you also need to make sure that the sections of your renga are connected. More than that, there should be some overall progression through the poem, perhaps moving from Point A at the start to Point B by the end. Or, a movement in time, say, from sunrise to sunset. Remember to revise carefully and thoughtfully for a better poem.

In Your Notebook

Although the renga is meant to be a collabora-
tive effort, there's nothing to stop you from writ-
ing your own renga. Some poets find it helpful
to have a sense of where their renga is going
before they begin. Others prefer to just start writ-
ing the linked poem and see what happens. I
suggest that you use the method that feels com-
fortable for you. In either case, begin with an
opening haiku. Revise it until it's just right. As you
rewrite, you might get a flash of what the next
two seven-syllable lines will be. Some young po-
ets I've worked with like to think of the renga as
a video that moves from one scene to the next.
Maybe that way of thinking will help you write
your own renga.

Write with a Partner

TANKA

Another poetic form that's related to the haiku is the *tanka*, which is a Japanese word meaning "short poem." The big difference between the haiku and the tanka, beyond the length of the poems, is that the tanka uses strong images to establish a mood. Beyond that, a tanka is usually thirty-one syllables written over five lines, making it look like a haiku plus two lines. In other words: 5–7–5–7–7. But don't get caught up on counting syllables. Like the haiku, a tanka has a "spirit" to it that should be the driving force of the poem. It's not just a poem that strictly contains a set number of syllables in each line.

Below is one of my tanka that should give you a good idea of what this poetic form looks like. Read it out loud a couple of times.

Lightning splits the sky
and for a moment we see
the empty playhouse
and just as suddenly
the yard is black again.

If you look closely at the poem, you'll see that it's divided into five lines, but the syllable count is 5–7–5–6–6, totaling twenty-nine syllables. Even though the syllable count is "off" a bit, the poem captures the spirit of a tanka by presenting a clear image that creates a certain mood. Another difference between the haiku and the tanka is that the tanka may include figurative language, like metaphors and similes, while the haiku will not. Finally, the tanka does not rely on the seasonal word as the haiku does.

When you write a tanka, make sure that you create an image and mood by using words that appeal to the senses. In this poem, I rely on the sense of sight to create an image. Read the poem again and see how I create the image of a dark night being momentarily brightened by a flash of lightning. And in that split second we see the empty playhouse. By using visual images, I tried to create a feeling of calm being disturbed.

Here are two other tanka. Read them over a few times, and then see if you can answer the questions that follow in your notebook.

Early October
a sugar maple ablaze
at the end of the pond
its fire reflected
in the still water.

The chestnut vendor
must shout to be heard above
the October winds
his words rise, sail away
like the thick smoke from his stove.

IMPROVE YOUR CRAFT #13:
Figurative Language

Metaphors and similes are both comparisons of dissimilar things, but similes use *like* or *as*. Here's an example of a metaphor: *She's a feather!* A comparable simile would be *She's as light as a feather!* As you may remember, haiku generally do not include figurative language, like metaphors and similes. When you write a tanka, however, the extra lines and syllables give you some room to include some figurative language. The right metaphor or simile can do wonders for the image that you are trying to create in your poem.

If you look back at my tanka on the bottom of page 85, you'll see I use this simile:

his words rise, sail away
like the smoke from his stove

Can you see how I use the sense of sight — *seeing the smoke sail away* — to show how the vendor's words vanish? That simile gives the reader a clearer image. Remember that a good comparison can make the images in your poem more vivid.

In Your Notebook

List the words and phrases in each poem that are connected to one of your senses: sight, smell, sound, taste, and touch. Next to each word, write down which sense it is connected to. Can you get a sense of the mood or feeling that each poem creates?

Another important difference between haiku and tanka is that the tanka does not rely on a "moment" the way the haiku does. The tanka may begin with a haiku moment, that time when something stops you in your tracks. But it goes beyond that moment. It allows the poet to think about the scene and the mood of the poem, and to work on the poem's flow.

Although a tanka doesn't need a seasonal setting, I'd suggest that you try to include the seasonal aspect in your tanka, at least when you write your first batch of tanka. Why? First, you might be able to use one of your haiku as a starting point for your tanka. In other words, start with the haiku and see if you can revise it and/or add to it to make it a tanka. But please remember that a tanka is not merely a haiku that you've stretched into a tanka. Don't just add syllables or words that do not create a good tanka.

Another reason for including a seasonal setting is that it will help you be specific as you write. If you look out a window in your school and see dandelions scattered across the soccer field, that bit of spring is a good way to start your poem. However, the seasonal aspect is not necessary in a tanka.

Another helpful tip for writing a tanka is to write a scene that you can visit. Writing about an imaginary scene is okay, but I think you'll be better off if you begin your tanka writing with a real scene. Go to that scene and observe. Don't just *look* at the scene. Observe. Notice. Take notes in your writer's notebook. As you write down your observations, are there any comparisons that come to mind? Are the dandelions like gold coins spread across the field? Once you think you have taken enough notes, underline the words and phrases that make the image come alive. They will more than likely be the words and phrases that appeal to your senses. You will want to consider these sense words and phrases when you draft your tanka.

After you write a draft of your tanka, take a good look at it and see if there is anything that you think could be better. Maybe your description isn't clear enough. Maybe some of your words are dull. Make any changes in your poem that you think will make it better. When you have made your changes, tuck the poem away. Give it some quiet time in a file folder or on your hard drive. After a few days — give it more time, if you can — go back to your poem and read it over a couple of times. Do you hear anything that needs work? If not, consider these checkpoints as you revise your poem:

CHECKLIST OF TANKA INGREDIENTS

* Does your tanka come close to the syllable count that I mentioned earlier: 5–7–5–7–7? Remember that the poem does not need to exactly follow this formula.

* Has your tanka created the feeling that you were aiming for? See if you can underline the parts of the poem that create that feeling.

✳ Does your tanka contain strong, clear images? Can you see the scene in the poem? To make sure, underline the words that create that image.

✳ Have you used any figurative language in your tanka? It's not necessary to include such language in a tanka, but the right metaphor or simile can make your poem stronger.

Write with a Partner

Sometimes writers get so caught up in their work that they overlook some of the essentials. Your writing partner can help by checking your work.

When you think your tanka is ready to be read by your writing partner, ask her to read through it a couple of times and check it against the Checklist of Tanka Ingredients on pages 89 and 90, looking for things like syllable count, feeling, images, and figurative language. Beyond that, she can also give you her overall feeling about your poem. Even though it follows the basics, it might be missing something that your writing partner may be able to spot.

OTHER SHORT POEMS

SYNONYM POEMS

Before you can write a good synonym poem, you need to know what a synonym is. A synonym is a word that means the same thing or almost the same thing as another word. For example, here are some synonyms for *small*: *petty, trivial, trifling, negligible, paltry, picayune, piddling.* Now you have to admit, there are some great words on that list. My favorites are *picayune* and *piddling.* I like the sounds of these words. Read these synonym poems and see how synonyms are used in them.

Food
Grub, chow, a sizable snack
It rescues me from a hunger attack

Large
Huge, titanic, just plain big
One such creature was Wilbur the pig.

Sad
Forlorn, bummed, or feeling small
It's often cured by a trip to the mall.

Ideas
Zany, foolish, crazy, too
Your best ideas come out of the blue.

There are a couple of things that make synonym poems work, and I bet you noticed some of them in these poems. A synonym poem:

- is one **couplet** (two lines of poetry that rhyme are called a couplet);
- has a first line that contains three or four synonyms for the subject of the poem, although you could use words that describe the subject;
- has a second line that describes the subject a little more (e.g., *One such creature was Wilbur the pig*) or tells how you feel about the subject (e.g., *It's often cured by a trip to the mall*);
- has about seven or eight syllables in each line, and they are arranged in a way that gives both lines similar rhythm.

As with all poems you write, you need to resign yourself to revising your work. Some writers I know revise as they go along. They might write a few lines of poetry, then go back and look for places that can be improved. This slows you down, but some writers like to fix a problem as soon as they spot it. Others wait until the entire first draft is written before they give much thought to revising the poem.

When you are writing a synonym poem, you can make some simple revisions by listening to the rhythm of your first line. Sometimes you can revise an awkward sounding line of poetry by changing the order of the words. That sometimes improves the sound of the line. For example, *Sweet and tender, nice enough* has a smoother rhythm than *Tender and sweet, nice enough.*

Pay attention to the end rhyme. If you love your second line but it doesn't rhyme with the first line, try looking for a new word to use at the end of the first line. You might, in fact, already have the word in that line, but it just needs to be moved to the end of the line. For example, in "Sad" I had drafted the poem so that *bummed* was the last word of the first line. But when I liked the second line so much, I moved *feeling small* to the end of that line.

One way to make your synonym poem funny is to write a second line that surprises the reader. The line should fit in the poem and make sense, of course. But if it's a surprise, you might get a laugh from the reader. For example, see how the second line of this synonym poem is a surprise:

Little Brother
Sweet and tender, nice enough
I hate it when you go through my stuff.

Below are a few first lines of synonym poems. See what you can come up with to complete each poem. The second line of a synonym poem should tell how you feel about the subject or describe it further. Try to include a surprise in the second line. That will make your poem funnier. After you've completed these synonym poems, try to write your own.

Happy
Blissed and cheerful, filled with glee

Cat
Feline, purrer, furniture scratcher

_____

Friends
Caring, helpful, full of advice

_____

Bugs
Flying, buzzing, annoying at night

_____

Family Vacation
Driving, arguing, moments of quiet

_____

IMPROVE YOUR CRAFT #14:
Using Synonyms

A thesaurus is a book of synonyms. As I mentioned at the start of this guide, you should have a good paperback thesaurus on your desk whenever you're writing. It can be especially helpful when you're writing a synonym poem. If you look up *happy* in a thesaurus, for example, you're likely to find works like these: *delighted, glad, pleased, contented, gratified, satisfied, elated, thrilled, tickled, cheerful, sunny, blithe, lighthearted, buoyant, carefree.* They all mean, more or less, the same thing as *happy,* so most of these words would be suitable to include in a synonym poem with a title of "Happy." However, if you read the list out loud, you'll notice how some words have more syllables than others. And the accents fall on different syllables in different words. For example, *gratified* and *contented* each contain three syllables, but the accent in *gratified* is on the first syllable while in *contented* it's on the second syllable. *Tickled, cheerful, carefree,* and *sunny* each have two syllables, and in each word the accent falls on the first syllable.

So, when you use a thesaurus to find synonyms for your synonym poem, you'll need to pay attention to syllable count and accent in the words you select, making sure that they do not disrupt the rhythm of each line.

In Your Notebook

If you keep your notebook close at hand, you can easily make lists of great words that might work well in a synonym poem. You can even write a short list of synonyms for those words. Remember that some words make better subjects for synonym poems than others. Adjectives and nouns are the most likely candidates. Also look for words that mean something to you. For example, *friends* and *family* might work for you. But remember what I said above: You can make a poem funny if you surprise your reader with the second line.

A good way to brainstorm words is to create a web. The center of the web will be the word for which you want synonyms. From there, you can branch out and write your synonyms in branches coming off the main topic. Here are a couple of webs that you can finish:

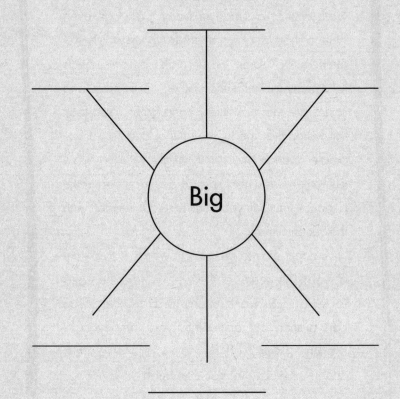

Big

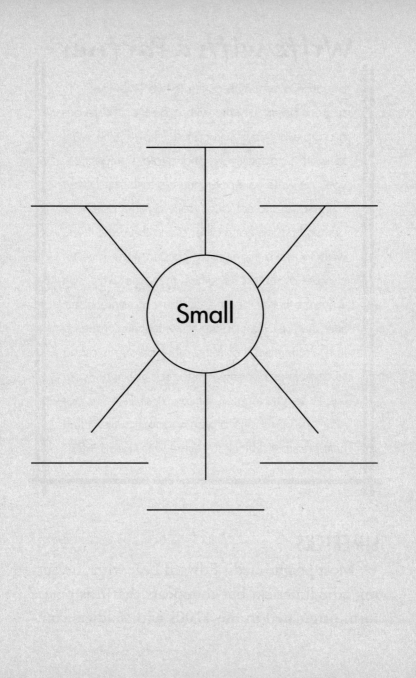

Write with a Partner

Because a synonym poem is two lines long, it's a great poem to write with a partner. There are a couple of ways you can do that. If you want to work cooperatively and avoid competition, you can write your poem the old-fashioned way: Choose a subject and work on the poem together, helping each other along the way. If you want to make things more challenging, you can choose a subject together, then see who can write the better poem. Or you can write a first line, then ask your partner to write the concluding line. Remember that if the other person is going to complete a poem you started, you want your line to be challenging but fun. And it's no fun for either of you if one of you chooses a word that is impossibly difficult to rhyme with. Keep it fun.

LIMERICKS

Most people credit Edward Lear with "inventing" the limerick, but it appears that this poetic form originated in the 1700s with soldiers coming home to Limerick, Ireland, after fighting a war in France. Regardless of how it started, good limericks are great fun to read and write. Here are a few of my limericks:

There was a young lady from Spain
Who went for a dance in the rain
Her tutu got wet
Though she did forget
And danced merrily up the lane.

I once knew a man named Bill
Who seemed always to need a pill
The pains in his head
Confined him to bed
And he slowly slipped downhill.

A poodle that barked through the night
Though cute was never polite
She kept me awake
Never gave me a break
Though I shouted with all my might.

I once knew a friend of the czar
Whose jacket I found quite bizarre
But he kept it so neat
From collar to seat
Until he got sick in the car.

If you read these limericks out loud — and you should do that often so you can really hear the music of a poem — you will hear a distinctive rhythm or bounce for which the limerick is famous. Lines 1, 2, and 5 are longer than lines 3 and 4. The longer lines have three accented (or stressed) syllables, like this: *I **once** knew a **friend** of the **czar**.* The shorter lines have two accented syllables, like this: *From **collar** to **seat**.* You will find that most limerick lines follow this pattern of accented syllables. (Remember that patterned rhyming poems will not follow all of the rules all of the time.)

This poem has a rhyme scheme that we show like this: *aabba.* This means that lines 1, 2, and 5 end with the same sound, and lines 3 and 4 end with the same sound, although a sound that's different from the one that ends lines 1, 2, and 5. The lowercase letters that we use to note rhyme schemes show which end words sound alike. (It doesn't mean that the three long a lines, for example, end with a long "a" sound, like *day, play,* or *delay.*)

When you write limericks, remember that they tell a story and your story isn't complete until the final word. I've met many students who did a great job writing the first four lines of a limerick but were satisfied with a fifth line that followed the rhythm and rhyme of lines 1 and 2 but didn't complete the story. Take another look at the first four lines of this limerick. Below it, I have written five fifth lines that do not complete the poem, even though they "fit" into the poem.

I once knew a man named Bill
Who seemed always to need a pill
The pains in his head
Confined him to bed
_____?_____

- Until he sat on the sill
- Because he always was ill
- Where he wrote poems with a quill
- Where the air was always so still
- And he wished he could cook on his grill

When you write your limerick, make sure that the final line completes the story you're telling and doesn't merely follow the "rules" of writing a limerick.

It goes without saying, but I can't resist saying it: As you work on your drafts and their revisions, make sure that you read the poem out loud. You can read it when you're alone. Better yet, you can read it to your writing partner to see if she can follow it. You can also try to get a chuckle from her, or at least a grin.

IMPROVE YOUR CRAFT #15: *Rhythm*

For most of the poems in this guide, syllable count is more important than rhythm. But a good limerick follows a form, and part of that form is the rhythm. A good tip for writing a limerick is to read it out loud every step of the way. Don't be bashful. The limerick has one of the most recognizable rhythms in poetry, so read yours aloud and listen for the rhythm of the limericks in this section. If your limerick doesn't have this distinctive rhythm, you'll need to make some changes. It could be that line 3 or 4 is too long. Or, maybe that an accent or two falls in the wrong place.

There are a couple of things you can do to try to fix the problem. The first is to see if you can change the word that presents the problem. Consult your thesaurus. See if you can find a suitable word as a replacement. Chances are, you can. If not, then you'll need to make other changes, like tinkering with word order or changing the idea of your poem. Don't worry if you find that altering the original idea of your poem is the only way to fix it. That's what revision is all about. Time spent fixing the rhythm of a limerick is time well spent.

In Your Notebook

One way to get started writing a limerick is to start with the first two lines — the opening couplet — because that can put you into the swinging rhythm of the limerick. Plus, writing the first two lines will give you a good start to the "story" of the limerick. Below are a few opening lines. See what rhyming line you can come up with to complete the couplet. Remember: The line you write must make sense. It should advance the story that I introduce in the first line. You can write your lines in your notebook.

1. There once was a man from France
2. There was an old lady with beads
3. An old man who recovered from mumps
4. There once was a boy with a book
5. A lady who ate lots of bread

If you have trouble coming up with a rhyming line for any of these, try writing your own opening couplet.

Complete one of the limericks that you started in your brainstorming work. Remember that your limerick must tell a story. Even though the story will be silly, it must make sense. If you still need practice before you write your own limerick, try to supply the missing lines for these limericks:

There once was a man in the gym
Who, at every chance, sang a hymn
He hit sour notes
That frightened the goats
_____?_____

There was an old lady from Maine
Who always stood out in the rain
_____?_____
_____?_____
Until she was washed down the drain.

A poodle with a bow in her hair
Would always lounge in my chair
She hated to move
She didn't approve
_____?_____

Write with a Partner

Most limericks start with something like *There once was a . . .* or *There was a . . .* But as you can see from my examples, I've used a couple of variations: *I once knew a man named Bill* and *I once knew a friend of the czar.* Brainstorm some alternatives with your writing partner. Don't be surprised if they pop into your head when you least expect them, like during study hall or when you're cleaning your room. It's like getting a song stuck in your head. Here are a few alternative opening lines for you to consider.

- My dad can be very kind
- A friend of mine drove his new car
- The monster that had curly hair
- A boy who liked hot dogs and beans
- A man I once knew in the city

CLERIHEWS

During World War II, a man named Edmund Clerihew Bentley wrote a regular column for a London newspaper. In the column he included a four-line humorous poem about a celebrity. Although Bentley frequently wrote about contemporary political figures, many of his poems were about historical characters, like writers, rulers, and politicians. Since Bentley invented this type of poetry, he named it after himself: Clerihew. (Well, if you invented a poetic form, wouldn't you want to name it after yourself? I know I would!) When I tried to write clerihew, I came up with these:

Britney Spears
Is just as calm as she appears
With all of her dough
She can afford to go with the flow.

"The Lord of the Rings"
To its fans means many things
But the movie producers offer thanks
Every time they visit their banks.

Harry Potter
Was a magical plotter.
At Hogwarts he became a master
After many a goof and disaster.

Huckleberry Finn
There's no end to the trouble he got in
No matter what his aunt had to say
He just wanted to get away.

As I mentioned above, the clerihew is a humorous four-line poem. (A four-line stanza or poem is called a **quatrain**.) But beyond that, you might notice that those four lines are really two couplets. What else do you notice about the poems? The first line of a clerihew is always the name of a famous person. This means, of course, that you need to rhyme with that person's name (which might explain why I've had so few clerihew written about me). The other ingredient of a clerihew is its **tone**. In other words, what attitude does the poet have toward the subject? The clerihew is meant to poke *gentle fun* at someone famous. If you look at the poem about Huck Finn, you see that I make fun of the fact that he's always in trouble. In the clerihew about *The Lord of the Rings*, I say that the producers are just happy about all the money the film made.

Note that I emphasize *gentle fun* because I want to make sure that you write your clerihew in the spirit of fun and not in the spirit of being mean. There's enough meanness in the world already. We don't need to add to it by writing nasty poems about people. Have fun when you write your clerihew, but remember: gentle fun.

When you're trying to decide who to write about, think "celebrity." But that's a relative term.

A celebrity can be someone that you see on TV or in the movies. But it can also be a local person, like the principal of your school or a neighbor who is known for his famous roses. Before you write your clerihew, give some thought to the subject. Make sure you pick someone that has a trait or quality that you can poke gentle fun at. For example, your principal might have a habit of wearing flashy ties or hamming it up whenever he makes announcements. Those might be traits that you want to include in your poem. But if he's an ordinary guy and an okay principal, he probably wouldn't make a good subject for your clerihew.

A good place to look for ideas is the bookstore. Browse the magazine section and see if you can come up with any good ideas. Look for magazines about sports figures, soap opera stars, musicians, and writers. Bring your notebook. I'll bet that you will find many people about whom you can write clerihew.

IMPROVE YOUR CRAFT #16:
Working with Rhyme

One of the most challenging parts of writing a clerihew is finding a word that rhymes with the subject of the poem, which happens to be a person's name. If you're stuck for a rhyme, you might want to consider using a rhyming dictionary. Your school library should have one. But you may want to invest in your own copy. (Scholastic offers a good paperback rhyming dictionary through its book clubs, so keep your eye open whenever you get the monthly book club flyer.)

A rhyming dictionary is a fun book. The entries are arranged in alphabetical order by sound rather than by the spelling of individual words. So, the guide "words" at the top of the page will look like this: *oodle-ool, ipe-iper, eery-eet,* and *uttle-uzzle.* If you want to find words that rhyme with *hat,* for example, you'd turn to the page with words that have the *at* sound, and you'll find a number of single syllable words like these: *at, bat, brat, cat, chat, fat, flat, gnat, mat, pat.* But you'd also find multi-syllabic words like these: *combat, chitchat, doormat, format, nonfat, tomcat, acrobat,* and *'fraidy cat.*

While a rhyming dictionary offers lots of rhyming words, if you read the words carefully, you might find a new idea for your poem. Suppose, for example, you think you want to write a poem about dogs, so you look up words that rhyme with *poodle*. You find, among others, *noodle* and *strudel*. Suddenly, you decide that your poem's not going to be about dogs. It's going to be about food! Of course, you could always have your poodle eating strudel or preparing noodles. A rhyming dictionary will open up lots of poetic possibilities for you.

In Your Notebook

Who can you write a clerihew about? It might help to begin by brainstorming some ideas, starting with general categories of celebrities. You might want to make a diagram like the one below.

Category	Names
Sports	
TV	
Movies	
Authors	
Musicians	

Once you have brainstormed possible subjects for your clerihew, you can make a quick web of one of the subjects. Draw a circle in the middle of a page in your notebook. Write the name of the subject in that circle. Then draw spokes coming from that circle with a smaller circle at the end of each spoke. In each of those circles write one quality, characteristic, or quirk of the subject. (A quirk, in case you didn't know, is a nifty noun that means "an individual knack or peculiarity.") Make sure you include specifics in your web. It might look like this:

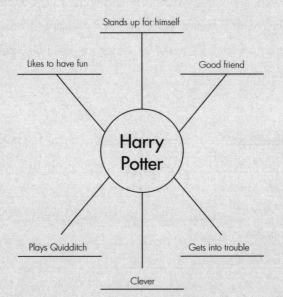

When you've written in some traits of your subject, see if you can find one or two especially good ones that you can include in your poem. Remember that you are not trying to be mean.

Before you try drafting your clerihew, see what you can rhyme with the names of the celebrities on the list below. You don't need to write the entire line that would follow the celebrity's name — coming up with some rhyming words would be enough for this exercise. Write your rhymes in your notebook.

Barry Bonds
George W. Bush
Han Solo
Jennifer Lopez
Orlando Bloom

When you're ready to draft your clerihew, remember that the first line contains only the person's name. The second line must rhyme with the subject's name. And the whole poem pokes gentle fun at the subject.

Write with a Partner

The clerihew is probably one of the best poems for having a lot of fun working with a partner. Grab your notebooks and start tossing out names of famous people who might make great clerihew subjects. When you come up with a good list, see what you and your partner have to say about somebody on the list. Why is that person famous? Does that person have a flamboyant way of doing something? If you want to hang onto your ideas, draw some webs in your notebooks. Then you can take your time writing without worrying about forgetting your stupendous ideas. If you or your partner is a good artist, try illustrating your poems with drawings of your subjects.

You can also cut out pictures of famous people from magazines and newspapers or you can download pictures and paste them into a section of your notebook. Paste your pictures in a way that leaves you room on the page to take notes or maybe write a draft of a clerihew. If you're a real people watcher, you might even want to have a separate notebook just for pasting pictures.

DISPLAYING YOUR POEMS

There are many places where you can display your poems. You may want to put them on the wall in your room. Or with your teacher's permission, you can showcase them in your classroom. When choosing a place, make sure that enough people will stroll by and read your poetry.

POSTER

Earlier I suggested that you look through magazines and art books for pictures that might inspire you to write haiku. A good way to display your haiku is to couple your poems with pictures on a poster. You can cut out pictures from magazines or draw your own illustrations to go with your poem. Since it might look a little odd to have a three-line poem and a picture on a large poster, you can either (a) use a smaller sheet of paper for your poster, or (b) put several related haiku on one poster. For example, you might have four or five good haiku about the summer. Why not put them on a poster along with a summer picture? Or you might have a few haiku about your neighborhood. They could be on one poster, too.

Use your imagination to come up with other artistic poster designs.

QUILT

To make a quilt, you'll need blank sheets of white paper. Copier paper works well. You can use colored paper, too, as long as it's light enough for you to see your haiku when you write them on the paper. Each sheet of paper will be a panel of the quilt and will contain one haiku. Before you write your haiku on the sheets, you need to get the paper ready for the quilt design. To do that, use a pencil to mark the middle of each side of the sheet of paper with a dot. Then join the dots such in a way that you get a diamond, like this:

To make your panel, write the haiku in the middle of the diamond. You can't leave small triangles at the corners of the diamond empty, so you can fill those spaces with appropriate drawings and designs. For example, if your haiku is about the basketball court down the street from your apartment, you can draw basketball items in each triangle. Maybe you'd draw a basketball, a hoop, a sneaker, and a ref's whistle.

To make your quilt, I suggest you use twenty panels arranged in five rows of four panels each. Writing twenty good haiku may take you some time, so it's a good idea to design and build a quilt with a friend or two. Although the quilt will look great on your wall, it might also look great on the wall of your grandmother's living room or your mother's office.

POETRY MINI-FLAGS

With 4x6-inch file cards, you can easily make great poetry mini-flags to decorate your room. If you want to add color to your flags, you can use pastel-colored copier paper that can be cut in half to make two 8½ x 5½ inch flags per sheet.

To make these mini-flags, simply turn your file card or sheet of paper so that the short side is at the top and bottom. Then, use a paper punch to punch two holes at the top of the flag, so it looks like this:

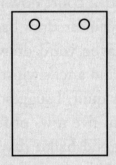

On each flag you can write a poem and draw or paste a picture above it or below it.

You can also organize your flags according to theme or type of poem. For example, you can create a string of poems about nature or celebrities. Or you can write haiku or clerihew.

ACCORDION BOOK

I like to make accordion books because they are easy to make and don't require stitching. An accordion book is a long strip of paper that folds into panels for pages. To make one, take a sheet of copier paper and divide it into eight panels like this:

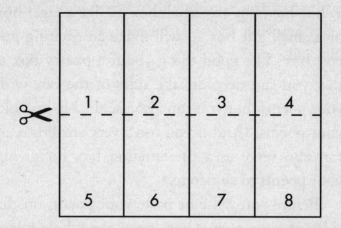

Notice that I have numbered each "page." Next, cut the sheet on the dotted line. Then tape page 5 along the edge of page 4 and fold on each solid line so the strip becomes an accordion. These folds will give you sixteen pages to write short poems on because you can write a poem on both sides of each page.

When you make an accordion book, don't forget to add artwork. You can make page 1 an eye-catching cover. You can also include a small drawing or design on each page. Or, you can add full-page illustrations related to the poems throughout the book.

POETRY SHOE BOX

It should be easy for you to get your hands on a shoe box, but any small box — like a cigar box or a small gift box — will make an exciting poetry box. The good thing about a poetry box is that you can decorate the sides of the box with your poems, but you can also use the box to hold your poems. (And if you use a very small box, it can also serve as a presentation box for giving your poems to someone.)

Before you write or paste your poems on the sides of your poetry box, paint the whole box a light color, like white or yellow. Or you can paint each panel of the box a wild color. Painting the panels of the box will make your poems stand out. With a nice coat of paint and your poems boldly presented on the sides of the box, this makes a great display of your talent.

GIVING YOUR POEMS

One of the things I like best about writing poems is giving them to other people. And because haiku are so short, you can give them as gifts in many different ways. Before starting any of these projects, get a supply of different colors and textures of paper. Visit a stationery store or an art-supply store and you'll find plenty of paper to choose from.

BOOKMARK

Cut out a few bookmarks from fancy, colorful paper. Make each one a convenient size. Something like 1½ x 6 inches is a good size, but use your imagination. Turn each bookmark sideways and carefully print your poem on one side. Or you can use heavier, textured watercolor paper for a bookmark. You can even paint a small design at the top of the bookmark and write your poem below that. If you really want to get fancy, you can punch a hole at the top of a bookmark and string some ribbon or yarn through it.

CARD

Any good art-supply store will sell blank cards, which are big enough to write a short poem on. You can even cut a blank card in half and get two small cards, which are perfect for short poems. (Personally, I like to give haiku on small cards.) You can decorate the front of the card and write your poem inside. Of course, if you have some nice paper, you can cut out your own cards and dress up the edges by cutting them with scissors that cut fancy edges.

POSTCARDS

Art-supply stores are likely to sell blank postcards made out of watercolor paper. Divide one side into halves: One half will be for a message and the other for the address. The other side of the postcard will be blank, and that's where you can write a haiku or two. Or you can draw a picture on that side, and write your poem in the message space on the other side. Although you can hand the postcard to a friend, most people I know love to get a good poem in the mail.

POETRY TAGS

You can buy shipping tags in an office supply store, or you can make your own. They are simply blank cards with a hole at one end. A string that you use to tie the tag to an item comes through the hole. They are sold in different sizes, although I like to use tags that are 2½ x 4½ inches. You can also make your own tags out of blank, colored file cards. Write your poem on one side of the card and put a drawing on the other side. Then tie it to your friend's backpack or desk. Or you can tie one to your mother's or father's briefcase.

POETRY CRACKER

With colorful wrapping paper and ribbon, you can present a poem to someone in a way that will be remembered for a long time. Write your poems on a sheet of paper and roll it up. You might want to put a rubber band around it or hold it together with a small piece of tape or one of your favorite stickers. Then wrap your rolled-up poem with wild wrapping paper and tie each end with some complementary ribbons. There you have it: a poetry cracker!

POCKET NOTEBOOK

If you have many short poems to give, but you don't have the time to make a fancy book, you could easily turn a pocket notebook into a gift book. Although you can buy different types of pocket notebooks, I recommend a spiral note-book for your gift book because over time, the pages are likely to fall out of the notebooks that are glued. Pick a notebook with a cover that has a cool color but has minimum print on it. You can cover whatever print there is with stickers. You can also paste a small drawing on the cover. Once you are set with the cover, you can very neatly write or print one poem on each page of your gift book. With some patience and care, it will be a treasure.

Don't limit yourself to my suggestions. I'm sure you can think of other ways of giving your poetry to your family and friends. And one of the best things about trying to come up with new, neat ideas is experimenting to see which ones will work. Get together with a writing partner and brainstorm other ways to make a gift of your poetry.

CONCLUSION

I hope the exercises and examples in this book gave you the confidence to write your own poetry. Do you have a writer's notebook bursting with ideas, drafts, and final versions of some great short poems? Maybe you've even given a few poems to someone dear to you.

As you continue to write poetry — no matter what kind of poem you choose to write — remember a few things:

- Try to write regularly. Set aside some time and a space — every day if you can — to relax and play with language.
- Be a keen observer. Look carefully at the world around you. Look deeply at the world inside you.
- Take chances when you write. Remember that you are writing for you.
- Be a careful reviser. Your poems will only be as good as the effort you put into making them good enough to satisfy you.

- Share your poems (if you want to). What could be a better gift than a poem that you worked hard on?
- Have fun! When you write a poem for yourself, you should have a good time with it.
- Work hard. I know this might seem to contradict what I just said — "Have fun" — but it doesn't have to. It takes hard work to write a good poem. But when you write for yourself, the work should be more fun than plain drudgery.

So grab that favorite pen of yours and your special writer's notebook, and keep writing!

ANSWERS

From page 29

2. If you read the poems with attention, you probably noticed that Buson sees the leaves being driven by the wind, Issa notices the crescent moon, Basho notices flowers leaning toward the sun, and Shiki notices water in the bright flash of lightning.

3. Buson and Issa pause at the end of the first line. They even use punctuation — a comma and a dash — to indicate a pause. Basho's pause is a little more subtle, but I'd say it comes after the second line. Like Buson and Issa, Shiki pauses at the end of the first line and helps us recognize that by using a colon. If you can't hear where the poets pause, try reading their haiku out loud. Reading poetry aloud is a great way to hear elements of a poem, like pauses, that we might miss when we read the poem to ourselves.

4. Buson's reference to fallen leaves tells us that his poem was written about autumn. Issa refers to the cold, so we can figure that this is a winter poem. Basho mentions May. With his ref-

erence to lightning, we know that Shiki is writing about a summer haiku moment.

From page 39
Her mailbox
leans into the honeysuckle
rusted and empty

Garry Gay

Between the lace curtains
the white cat's eyes
follow a snowflake

Doris Heitmeyer

after the storm
I cannot find
the snowman's eyes

Denise Coney

From page 41
<u>per</u>-son-al
en-cy-clo-<u>pe</u>-di-a
<u>win</u>-dow
out-<u>stand</u>-ing
su-per-in-<u>ten</u>-dent

<u>qui</u>ck
<u>al</u>-man-ac
<u>sing</u>
se-<u>lec</u>-tion
ri-<u>dic</u>-u-lous
dis-<u>cov</u>-er-y
re-<u>turn</u>

From page 42
The "lone firefly" tells us that this haiku takes place during the summer. In the second haiku, "cold wind" may at first lead us to think that the poem is set in winter. But the second line — "just-swept leaves" — tells us that it is autumn, when leaves fall from the trees.

From page 51
In the poem by George Swede,
What = crows sitting under a scarecrow
Where = in a field or garden
When = summer (because of the lightning)

In the poem by Bernard M. Aaronson,
What = pink magnolia blossoms scattered on the lawn

Where = in a yard
When = late spring or early summer

In the poem by Penny Harter,
What = cellar rats
Where = in a cellar
When = winter